# DEAR INSECURITY

A Woman's Guide To Release Self-Doubt And Boldly Activate Your God-Given Gifts

Crystal S. Daye

**DEAR INSECURITY.** Copyright © 2021. Crystal S. Daye. All Rights Reserved.

Printed in the United States of America.

No portion of this book may be reproduced, stored in a retrieval system, or transmitted in any form or by any means, except for brief quotations in printed reviews, without the prior written permission of DayeLight Publishers or Crystal S. Daye.

**ISBN: 978-1-953759-27-6 (paperback)**

Scripture quotations marked "KJV" are taken from the Holy Bible, King James Version (Public Domain).

Scripture quotations marked (NIV) are taken from the Holy Bible, New International Version®, NIV®. Copyright © 1973, 1978, 1984 by Biblica, Inc.™ Used by permission of Zondervan. All rights reserved worldwide.

Scripture quotations marked "NASB" are taken from the New American Standard Bible®, Copyright © 1960, 1962, 1963, 1968, 1971, 1972, 1973, 1975, 1977, 1995 by The Lockman Foundation. Used by permission.

Scripture quotations marked (NLT) are taken from the Holy Bible, New Living Translation, copyright © 1996, 2004, 2007 by Tyndale House Foundation. Used by permission of Tyndale House Publishers, Inc., Carol Stream, Illinois 60188. All rights reserved.

Scripture quotations marked "ESV" are from the ESV Bible® (The Holy Bible, English Standard Version®), copyright © 2001 by Crossway Bibles, a publishing ministry of Good News Publishers. Used by permission. All rights reserved.

Scriptures Quotations marked "GNB" or "GNT" are from the Good News Bible © 1994 published by the Bible Societies/HarperCollins

Publishers Ltd UK, Good News Bible © American Bible Society 1966, 1971, 1976, 1992. Used with permission.

GOD'S WORD is a copyrighted work of God's Word to the Nations. Quotations are used by permission. Copyright 1995 by God's Word to the Nations. All rights reserved.

Scripture and/or notes quoted by permission. Quotations designated (NET) are from the NET Bible® copyright ©1996-2016 by Biblical Studies Press, L.L.C. All rights reserved.

The Holy Bible, Modern English Version. Copyright © 2014 by Military Bible Association. Published and distributed by Charisma House. All rights reserved.

# Dedication

This book is dedicated to my mother, Nadine Gregory-Brown. Thank you for always believing in me and speaking life into my dreams no matter how "crazy" they sounded. Thank you for always "prophesying" that I was purposed to do more and be more, even when I could not imagine or believe it myself.

My greatest desire is that you will read this book and overcome your own insecurities and finally start living the life of purpose, impact, and abundance that God ordained for you.

# Acknowledgment

Special thanks to Stacy Samuels and C. Orville McLeish for helping me bring this book to life. I appreciate you very much.

To my prayer partners, amazing friends, wise mentors and clients, I love each of you and appreciate the continuous support.

My family, I love you endlessly.

To you who are reading this book, thank you for allowing me to share the lessons God has taught me on this faith journey. I pray you will be tremendously blessed and forever impacted.

# Table of Contents

Dedication **v**

Acknowledgment **vii**

Dear Insecurity **11**

Introduction **13**

**Chapter 1**

Accept Your Identity **17**

**Chapter 2**

Define Success for Yourself **31**

**Chapter 3**

Practice Forgiveness **39**

**Chapter 4**

Make Relationships A Priority **47**

**Chapter 5**

Discern Your Season **55**

**Chapter 6**

Journal the Vision **63**

**Chapter 7**

Become ~~Self-~~ GOD -Motivated **75**

**Chapter 8**
Be Still (Surrender) **85**

**Chapter 9**
Crying Is Allowed **95**

**Chapter 10**
Pursue Your Passions **103**

**Chapter 11**
Trust The Process **111**

**Chapter 12**
Level-Up Your Faith **117**

**Chapter 13**
Discover Your Gifts **125**

**Chapter 14**
Be Bold. Be Extra. Be Intentional **139**

**Chapter 15**
Becoming The Woman God Has Called You To Be **147**

**Chapter 16**
How To Consistently Overcome Insecurity **155**

**Conclusion 157**

**7 DAY FROM INSECURITY TO IMPACT CHALLENGE 161**

**About The Author 169**

# Dear Insecurity

For so long you have convinced me that I was not enough. Every time I wanted to step into what God has for me, I allowed you to keep me stuck. I looked at what others were doing and never accepted that there was more for me. Even though I had a desire for more, to do more, and be more, the imposter syndrome took me over, and I started to doubt my gifts and talents.

Sometimes you disguised yourself in perfectionism, and other times you resulted in procrastination, but whenever you showed up, I got stuck, doubtful, and crippled by my own feelings of inadequacy.

I remember when I was young and dreamed of doing big things, somehow as I grew older, you grew louder and I allowed you to have a greater hold on me.

Today I am choosing to WIN! I am choosing to let my faith grow bigger so I can silence you. Insecurity, you will no longer have a hold on me and on what God has in store for me.

Dear Insecurity, I am no longer afraid of being rejected because I know I am loved by God *(See 2 Timothy 1:7)*. I no longer doubt my abilities because I am called by God *(See Romans*

*8:29)*. I am no longer shrinking because I am fully equipped by God *(See Hebrews 13:21)*.

So, Dear Insecurity, GOODBYE!

# Introduction

When I started writing this book, I started praying for you. I started praying that, through the pages of this book, God will give you the breakthrough you need to truly activate your gifts and to boldly walk in all He has in store for you.

**So, let me ask, can you relate to any of these?**

- *Self-doubt*
- *Fear*
- *Anxiety*
- *Low Self Esteem*
- *Self-limitation*
- *Jealousy*
- *Inadequacy*
- *Comparison*
- *Complacency*
- *Anger*
- *Depression*
- *Discomfort*
- *Procrastination*
- *Self-criticism*

- *Small thinking*
- *Stop dreaming*
- *Fear of success*
- *Fear of failure*
- *Always seeking validation*
- *Constant people-pleasing*
- *Keep starting, but never finishing*
- *Feelings of unworthiness*
- *Mundane/living boring*
- *Feeling guilty for your successes*
- *Afraid to celebrate others*
- *Afraid to celebrate yourself*
- *Cannot take criticism*
- *Over apologizing*
- *Happy when others fail*
- *Unforgiving*

I can go on, but these are signs that you are struggling with insecurity.

Insecurity is an enemy to your purpose and impact.

In this book, I have shared some practical tools to help you release self-doubt so you can become motivated and discover your God-given gifts.

"

*We ask ourselves, 'Who am I to be brilliant, gorgeous, talented, fabulous?' Actually, who are you not to be? You are a child of God. Your playing small does not serve the world. We were born to make manifest the glory of God that is within us. It's not just in some of us; it's in everyone.*

— *Marianne Williamson*

"

# Chapter 1

# Accept Your Identity

*"But you are a chosen race, a royal priesthood, a holy nation, a people for his own possession, that you may proclaim the excellencies of him who called you out of darkness into his marvelous light." (1 Peter 2:9 – ESV).*

One day, while driving, I was talking to the Lord about my own insecurities. I started to ask Him why I am not as confident as others. I know many people see me on social media making moves and wonder how I do it, but I know that I am not very confident. There were so many times I would shrink back from doing things I truly wanted to do. In my mind, if I could become more confident, that would "cure" my insecurities. Then the Lord whispered, *"The antidote for insecurity is not self-confidence. It's actually identity, especially knowing who you are in Me."*

That resonated so much in my soul that I immediately called my friend and started to share with her all God was sharing with me. So I am writing this chapter to you as if you are my friends too. Honestly, this has probably been one of my biggest breakthroughs that have kept me focused on my purpose journey. I pray you will get your own breakthrough too!

## THE "CURE" FOR INSECURITY

If you are a Christian, there are some fundamentals we believe:

1. God is all-powerful
2. God is all-knowing
3. Nothing is impossible with God!

As flawed and imperfect human beings, we know we have many limitations, weaknesses, and yes, those ever-doubtful moments that hinder us from believing we can accomplish many of our dreams. Here is the cure: "If you stop looking at who you are and start believing who God has called you to be, then you can accomplish all the dreams He has placed in your heart."

> "If you stop looking at who you are and start believing who God has called you to be, then you can accomplish all the dreams He has placed in your heart."

**Perfect GOD + Imperfect Me = Unlimited Potential**

The key is to focus on **His abilities** more than *your inabilities.*

Listen, I do not know about you, but this makes me want to burst into a praise dance because I know my insecurities disappear when my focus is on God.

Let us look at some biblical examples:

1. David and Goliath - David was a small shepherd boy who went to the battlefield to take food for his brothers. David saw how terrified the Israelites were and was so embarrassed. He wondered why the Israelites were afraid of a giant that God created. David chose to focus on God's abilities and not his own weakness (that he was just a boy and not even a warrior). You know the rest of the story, right? Well, if you do not, read 1 Samuel 17. In the end, David won because He accepted who he was in God (his identity).

2. Queen Esther - Esther was an orphan. God used Esther's beauty to grant her favor, and she ended up being queen. Haman (an envious man) decided that he wanted to get rid of the Israelites. Esther's uncle, Mordecai, challenged her to approach the king to ask for help, but Esther was terrified because she could be killed to do such a thing. Esther realized she could not do it, so she and the other Israelites FASTED (they chose to focus on God's ability), and of course, her people were saved. Again, when Esther got stuck on her own "limitations," it posed a high probability of failure for her and her people. Instead, Esther trusted in who she was in God, and abundance became available.

3. Mary, Mother of Jesus – Picture being engaged to the love of your life, planning your wedding and life with your "boo," and then your life is interrupted with news

that you are pregnant (by the Holy Spirit as a virgin). Huh! What?

Stop here and read Luke 1:26-38 (even if you know the story, please re-read it and picture yourself as Mary).

Every time I read this story, I get jealous of Mary. Why? Somehow, despite her insecurities and possible considerations as to how she was chosen to bring the Savior of the world, would her fiancé still marry her, and how much would her life change; Mary's obedience to God is admirable. She simply said, "Yes, Lord."

I will be the first to admit that my first reaction is not always "Yes, Lord" when God tells me to do something. It is normally, "Lord, send me a confirmation, two or three please" or "Lord, me? Really? I don't think I am worthy, capable or equipped to do that" or "Lord, what will people say" or "Is that even You, Lord, because that must be the devil?"

Do not judge me as I am simply being honest. Can you relate?

Even though Mary was troubled, perplexed, and extremely shocked, she asked the Lord how it was even possible to have a baby when she had never had sex. Once the Lord assured her that it was by His might and not by her doing, she rested and believed.

Honestly, Mary must have been so secured about her identity in Christ. She must have known His voice, believed He is a good God with a great plan for her life, and trusted Him so much that she could respond in obedience and submission, even in her doubts.

Is that the level of assurance, faith, and confidence you desire on your journey towards being a purpose-driven woman? Do you want to be at this level where your insecurities and self-doubt dissolve once you hear God's voice because your desire to be obedient is greater than your perceived self-limitations?

Many will read this part of the book and think, "Well, I know a lot of non-Christians who have high self-confidence, who believe in themselves and have accomplished great things." I am sure there are times that you have accomplished things in your own strength, but why? This is so because we are all made in God's image so he has already deposited so much in us. Also, He has blessed us with gifts and wisdom that enable us to do "great" exploits without acknowledging Him.

> **Do you want to be at this level where your insecurities and self-doubt dissolve once you hear God's voice because your desire to be obedient is greater than your perceived self-limitations?**

Consider the story of the Tower of Babel in Genesis 11:1-9. The people wanted to build a tower that reached to heaven. God saw that He placed so much potential in them that they could actually accomplish this goal without Him, so He decided to confuse their language.

So I want to challenge you with this question, do you want to accomplish your goals or God's purpose?
Whether we want to accept it or not, most people are living the "best" life they can, based on their standards or the world's. However, true purpose can only be accomplished when you surrender your will and accept God's will. Most times, it looks different from how you envisioned it, but it will be the best and most fulfilling life ever.

Therefore, finally getting over insecurity really comes down to learning more and more about who you are in Christ, relying on Him to do all He wants through you.

Let us look at a practical example.

You know God is calling you to write a book, but you start saying, "I'm not good at English. Who would ever read my book? What will make my book different? I'm not really a writer, etc."

Insert your excuse here:

_____
_____
_____
_____

Instead of focusing on your inabilities, I challenge you to pray that God will anoint you to write. Believe that He knows why someone needs your message and truly allow "self" to die so that God can write through you. Remind yourself that you truly can do all things through Christ.

Your struggle might not be writing; it might be speaking in public, asking for a promotion, applying for a job you are not qualified for, launching a business or nonprofit organization, going back to school, among other things. Honestly, it does not matter your excuse for delaying what God has called you to do. It is firstly disobedience, so you need to repent. Secondly, it is a lack of trust in God. This means you are saying He is a liar because you do not believe He will have your best interest at heart at all times. Thirdly, delaying means you do not know who you really are in Christ, and you are not reading His Word to know what He has said about you.

These are hard things to accept, but each time I find myself struggling to do something, I return to the place of "dying to myself." If I did not practice this, I would not have written one book, not even to consider seven books. I would not have left my "nine to five" job and launched a publishing company that has given birth to hundreds of books for kingdom authors, and I would not have launched a podcast where people in over forty-five countries are being inspired by the Gospel, among other experiences.

While you may be tempted to think that this is Crystal's experience because she is "talented, gifted or called" or whatever else you may say, understand that this is not the case. Each time I step out to do something, I struggle with self-doubt, jealousy, feelings of not being good enough, and the belief that my past mistakes have denied me the right to be used by God. I look at the many "ordinary" people in the Bible who have made an amazing impact because they choose to ACCEPT THEIR IDENTITY instead of succumbing to their insecurity.

A few reminders of what God has said about you:

- He made you more than a conqueror through Christ (See Romans 8:37).

- He always leads you in triumph in Christ (See 2 Corinthians 2:14).

- He has given you everything you need for life and godliness (See 2 Peter 1:3).

- He has blessed you with every spiritual blessing (See Ephesians 1:3).

- The Holy Spirit helps you in your weaknesses (See Romans 8:26).

- His strength is perfected in your weakness (See 2 Corinthians 12:9).

- He forgives and cleanses you from every sin (See 1 John 1:9).

- He endues you with power from on high (See Acts 1:8).

- He works everything for good for those who love Him (See Romans 8:28).

I know that not everyone is called to stages or platforms, and not everyone will write books or launch podcasts. However, I am led to share that now God needs you where He has called you to serve - in your job, politics, agriculture, medicine, as a missionary, mother, Sunday school teacher, speech therapist, or an accountant. It does not matter. We are all struggling with something, but in our weakness, His strength is made perfect. If we surrender to His leading and operate in purpose, which leads to an eternal impact, then believe me that you will experience so much abundance that you will know it was not by your own might. This is where God gets all the glory.

## COACH YOURSELF

What are some areas in your life that you are struggling with insecurities?

_____
_____
_____
_____
_____
_____

**Dear Insecurity**

Identify two "ordinary" people you know who are pursuing their purpose and share how/why it inspires you.

_____
_____
_____
_____

What is one thing you would do presently if you were fearless or not struggling with any insecurity?

_____
_____
_____
_____

Write a letter entitled "Dear Insecurity" and use scriptures to tell "insecurity to go" (listen to my podcast *Diary of a Jesus Girl - Episode 2* as an example)

_____
_____
_____
_____
_____
_____

## KEY LESSONS

- The antidote for insecurity is knowing your identity.
- When you know who you are, you can walk boldly in your uniqueness.
- The only limitations that exist are the ones I have placed on myself.
- Perfect GOD + Imperfect Me = Unlimited Potential.

"

*Success is defined by a continuing desire to be the person God called you to be and to achieve those goals that God helps you to set.*

— *Charles Stanley*

"

## Chapter 2

# Define Success for Yourself

*"Keep this Book of the Law always on your lips; meditate on it day and night, so that you may be careful to do everything written in it. Then you will be prosperous and successful." (Joshua 1:8 – NIV).*

Many people go through life throwing their own pity parties because they spend their lives measuring success by comparing themselves to others.

As children, we begin to visualize our lives based on what we see or allow the culture to dictate what success means for us. Whether it means you must have a degree, drive a certain car, pursue certain

**To truly overcome insecurity and release self-doubt, we have to stop and evaluate what success for our lives look like.**

professions, acquire material possessions, get married, and so on, we are all guilty of allowing everything and everyone except God to define success for our lives.

To truly overcome insecurity and release self-doubt, we have to stop and evaluate what success for our lives look like. Someone will always be better at something and have more than you. You will always have a desire to accomplish more because that is how life is. The comparison game never ends. At the end of the day, you have to get to a place where you realize that success was God's idea in the first place.

I remember being in a small meeting with some amazing ladies who, in my view, were extremely successful. They had great careers, multiple degrees, were happily married, drove nice cars, lived in nice communities, and yes, they were saved. Honestly, comparing myself to them, I did not come near to their earthly accomplishments. The facilitator asked if we thought we were successful; to my surprise, I was the only person that said yes. The other ladies felt they needed to be married or did not like their jobs, or simply desired more. I came to the realization that my definition of success was different. Success for me simply means obeying God and walking in His will. Of course, I desire to achieve many things, but I have come to a place of contentment that Christ is truly enough.

It is great to have goals, use your gifts, have nice possessions and achieve your dreams, but I challenge you to not see success as just one thing but as a journey of progress. It is not just about what you do, but also who you become.

## ALIGN YOUR SUCCESS WITH YOUR CORE VALUES

When defining success for yourself, you need to get clear on your core values.

Values are considered principles that guides your life, dictate your behavior and help you understand what aligns to the core of who you are. When you live by your values, you will feel better about yourself and get more focused on doing the things that are important to you.

If you value your family, when you take on a job where you work 80 hours per week, you will always feel stressed and conflicted; or if you are a woman speaker with husband and children to take care of, you might not desire to hop on a plane four times per month to speak at events, as another woman speaker who is single.

If you value your relationship with God, you will struggle to take opportunities that causes you to compromise your faith.

You must learn to pause and do personal introspection so you can be clear on your personal values to help you define success for yourself.

Also, as you move through life, your core values may change. For example, when you start your career, success for you is how much money you make or climb up the corporate ladder. But after you have a family, work-life balance may be what you value more.

Identifying your core values are a central part of defining success for yourself. By becoming more aware of these, you can use them as a guide to make the best choice in any situation.

Many people chase after a version of success, only to find once they accomplish it, they are unhappy. They realize that what they had to sacrifice or do to accomplish it was out of alignment with who they are or who they desire to be.

I remember in 2017, I was speaking at an entrepreneurial event with some other accomplished women. One of the speakers spoke about her marriage failure as she was building her business. The other women in the room were saying "Ohh, wow! Sorry to hear." She said, "No, it was a sacrifice I was willing to make. My business was more important to me than that relationship." I was very shocked to hear this. But, in retrospect, I realized it was simply contradictory values.

I personally will never sacrifice my relationship for business; but guess what? I cannot judge because we all have different definition of what success looks and feels like for us.

Remember, you are unique; God's plan for you is unique. Therefore, you must never measure your success with someone else's ruler. If you do, you will accomplish all the things on your "list," yet struggle with living in peace, contentment, and abundance.

## COACH YOURSELF

How did you define success when you were a child?

_____

_____

_____


What is success for you now?

_____

_____

_____

_____

_____

_____


What area of your life have you compared your success to someone else?

_____

_____

_____

_____

_____

_____

**Dear Insecurity**

How would your life change if you truly started seeing success God's way versus the world's way?

_____

_____

_____

_____

_____

### KEY LESSONS

- Success should be defined by living in God's will.
- Do not allow the culture to dictate how you define success.
- Success is not just about achievement but also who you have become in the process.
- True success aligns with your values.

"

*To forgive is to set a prisoner free and discover that the prisoner was you.*

— *Lewis B. Smedes*

"

# Chapter 3

# Practice Forgiveness

*"Bear with each other and forgive one another if any of you has a grievance against someone. Forgive as the Lord forgave you." (Colossians 3:13 – NIV).*

We will have many experiences in this life, including betrayals, hurt, insensitivity, and just harmfulness towards us. In these moments of immense distress and injustice we experience, our human reaction is to have ill-feelings towards the individual or persons who have done us harm. These ill-feelings lead to bitterness, which leads to unforgiveness.

I have been in church long enough to hear many sermons on unforgiveness and its effects, yet no matter how many times this message is preached, the altar is normally filled with people who harbor unforgiveness in their hearts toward the person/s who would have hurt them. This is because forgiving someone is not the easiest thing to do. Why? Because we tend to believe the person does not deserve our forgiveness. It can feel like you are letting them "off the hook."

## WHAT REALLY IS FORGIVENESS?

Forgiveness is choosing to let go of thoughts of revenge and releasing any resentment you may have toward someone you felt has hurt you.

Forgiveness is a choice that you will have to make over and over again throughout your life. Choosing to forgive is exercising and extending goodness, even toward those who are not good to you.

Remember that forgiveness does not mean forgetting or excusing the hurt done to you or making up with the person. It is simply letting go of something that is hurting you so you can have peace to move on with your life.

The topic of forgiveness is now a medical topic as doctors have seen how unforgiveness has affected people's health very negatively (such as cancer, heart attacks, hypertension, among other illnesses).

Personally, I do not believe getting sick over anyone is worth it. No, I am not downplaying whatever you may have experienced that led to you feeling that bitterness or pain. Still, as they say, unforgiveness is holding you as a prisoner while the person walks around living their life unaffected by it.

Are you ready to forgive or not? Maybe you are or maybe you are not. Just remember it is a process, but it will give you peace and joy to move on with your life.

It is impossible to truly live a purpose-filled and joy-filled life when you are holding on to unforgiveness. Your blessings are on the other side of letting go off bitterness.

How do you forgive? **My biggest tip is to pray for the person.** Intentionally call the person's name to God and ask Him to help you release him or her. You cannot hate someone when you are praying for the person. I must warn you that it will be very hard to call their name and pray for them in the beginning. But, this is a notable indication that you have grievance toward someone if you cannot pray for the person. I will even challenge you to pray blessings for them. Sounds crazy, right? Do it! Believe me, it works. You might cry, scream, or even get upset while doing it, but keep praying every day until you find it easier to call the person's name.

> *"A forgiving lifestyle helps you become more like Christ. As you learn the importance of forgiveness and begin to practice forgiving others, your heart will heal from bitterness, and your personal growth will lead you to the promotions God has planned for you."*
> 
> *~ Joyce Myers*

**Dear Insecurity**

A few years ago, I was really bitter towards my daughter's father. The Lord knows that whenever I thought about him, the thoughts were very impure and downright evil. In my mind, he deserved something bad happening to him based on what he did to me. It was one of my spiritual mothers who shared that we should pray for the person who hurt us. I thought she was crazy, but I tried it anyway. For the first few days, all I could do was ask the Holy Spirit to intercede on my behalf because I did not think he deserved to be blessed. For weeks I kept praying for him, some days I cried, and other days I was angry. I realized that day by day, it got easier, and it was bearable. Then eventually, I started to tolerate him better. Now we are good, for the most part. Every now and then, though, I have to pray and start over the process.

Listen, I know it is hard, but it is for your good. So start praying for the person now.

### COACH YOURSELF

Name something you need to forgive your younger self for.

_____

_____

_____

_____

_____

_____

_____

Who do you need to forgive?

_____
_____
_____
_____
_____

Why do you think forgiveness is so important to living an abundant and impactful life?

_____
_____
_____
_____
_____

How do you know when you have truly forgiven someone?

_____
_____
_____
_____
_____

### KEY LESSONS

- Forgiveness benefits the forgiver (the person who experiences the hurt) more than the one who needs to be forgiven.
- Sometimes the person I need to forgive is myself!
- When you forgive, you actually become a better person.
- You cannot hate someone if you truly pray for them.

**"**

*Find a group of people who challenge and inspire you; spend a lot of time with them, and it will change your life.*
*— Amy Poehler*

**"**

Chapter 4

# Make Relationships A Priority

*"Be completely humble and gentle; be patient, bearing with one another in love. Make every effort to keep the unity of the Spirit through the bond of peace." (Ephesians 4:2-3 – NIV).*

God gives us the gift of relationships. Healthy relationships can encourage us, challenge us to be better versions of ourselves, help us through difficult times, and draw us closer to our Father.

> *"We can improve our relationships with others by leaps and bounds if we become encouragers instead of critics."*
> — Joyce Meyer

Maintaining healthy relationships with the people I love the most have been one of my biggest motivations in going after my dreams and goals. My family have been more than a blessing in every way. They support me, cheer me on, and accept my imperfections, weaknesses, and flaws without judgment.

Every day I am grateful for my family and friends. God has blessed me immensely with people who value me and who I love dearly.

Of course, I have experienced betrayals, disappointments, hurt, criticism, and personal attacks in various seasons of my life. However, I learnt the power of forgiveness very early in life, so I do not dwell in bitterness. I try not to hold on to toxic relationships; instead, I focus on those who truly matter.

I do not take for granted that you may or may not have a good relationship with your parents or have good friends and relatives. We are relational beings, and we were never meant to do life alone. Here is my challenge: if you do have people in your life who love, support, and value you, let them know often.

If you do not have people in your life who you trust and who appreciate you, it is not too late to pray about this. God will honor your prayers and align you with people who you can walk this life out with.

Remember, family is not always blood; you may have been adopted, grew up in a childcare facility, and so forth. However, you can find family at church, work, or school; sometimes, even your friends become your family.

In your ambitious pursuit of success and dreams, do not neglect relationships that matter. Whether it is your parents, siblings, spouse, children, mentors, mentees, or other individuals, having people in your life is a blessing, especially to share positive and difficult times with.

When it comes to insecurity, most times we struggle with the past criticism and labels placed on us by others. When we were younger, someone spoke against our dreams, attacked our identity. rejected us or made us constantly feel unworthy. Believe me, I know all too well the struggle of not feeling good enough based on what others have said. But the right relationships will foster love, appreciation and celebrate us. Having persons in your corner who cheer you on, encourage you when you are down, cry happy tears with you when you are winning or come down in the mud when you feel you have lost.

While we might want tons of people to do that, believe me, having one or two true solid family member, close friends, church mates or coworkers can be such a blessing.

Appreciate The Gift Of Family:

> *"Families are the compass that guides us. They are the inspiration to reach great heights and our comfort when we occasionally falter."*
>
> *— Brad Henry*

Cultivate Healthy Friendships:

> *"Best friends are the people in your life who make you laugh louder, smile brighter and live better."*
>
> — *Unknown*

### COACH YOURSELF

How can you better pursue healthy relationships?

_____

_____

_____

_____

How would your best friend describe you?

_____

_____

_____

_____

Who are the people who positively affect your life, and you would like to spend more time with?

_____

_____

What are some ways you can express your love and appreciation for your family/friends?

_____

_____

_____

_____

### KEY LESSONS

- Positive family relationships are built on quality time, communication, and appreciation for each other.
- A friend is someone who understands your past, believes in your future, and accepts you just the way you are.
- As you walk away from toxic relationships, you make space and find more emotional energy for healthy relationships.
- The relationships we experience with the people around us have a great influence on our wellbeing.

*"*

*Be aware of what season you are in and give yourself the grace to be there.*

— *Kristen Dalton*

*"*

## Chapter 5

# Discern Your Season

*"There is a time for everything, and a season for every activity under the heavens." (Ecclesiastes 3:1 – NIV).*

Let me start by first explaining what "discernment" means. In simple words, it means to examine, access, or prayerfully gain insight into a situation. Of course, spiritual discernment goes deeper but let us not complicate it now.

We are often going about life pursuing things that are not aligned with the season we are in. When it comes to purpose and impact, identifying your season is important, so you do not give up too easily or keep holding on when God wants to give you better.

Life takes us through different transitions. If you are stuck in a season that has ended, then you can miss the new things God wants to do in and through you. When it comes to your

## Dear Insecurity

passions, calling, or assignment, these things will change over different seasons.

Look at David. In one season, he was a shepherd boy tending sheep; next season, he was playing his harp to relieve Saul from the evil spirits tormenting him; next season, David was a warrior fighting on the battlefield; next season, he was a fugitive running for his life; and then another season, he was king. Similarly, you will also go through a series of beginnings and endings in your life.

In the Bible, we see various people of faith experiencing seasons of dryness when it seems as if everything is stagnant, then seasons of waiting that challenge our faith and prune us. There are seasons of fruitfulness where things get busy, and life feels more joyful; then we are hit with seasons of trials that feel like you cannot get a break from hardships. I am sure you can fill in the blanks that could describe other seasons you have experienced.

When we are in a particular season, we tend to believe that it will be our final destination. Sometimes it feels like the scarcity seasons are longer than the seasons of abundance. But it comes down to posture and perspective.

At the end of the day, God really cares more about our character than our comfort. If we can quickly discern the season we are in, it makes the faith journey more bearable (especially in the hard seasons).

Seasons change, it is a simple part of life, and we have no control over it. While we might not be able to understand it, there is always a reason for the season, and you have to be prayerful about how to operate.

The key to success is finding out the season you are in. Do not allow the enemy to convince you that any season is permanent. Instead, work on building your faith in God so you can learn the necessary lessons to prepare you for the next season.

Do not think the "present" inactivity of your life is an indication of your "future" progress.

Sometimes we have this false perception that life should always be about reaping. That is not possible. There must be a time to sow, and when you sow, it will take a while to see the fruit.

> **Do not allow the enemy to convince you that any season is permanent.**

Changing seasons can be scary, particularly since you would have gotten comfortable whether in hardship or abundance. As a result, when the season shifts, you remain stuck. Many times people get stuck in a hard season. The cycle keeps repeating because they are not willing to do or be different and gracefully walk into their next season.

Do not stay stuck in a past season or get fixated on a future one; you will miss the one you are currently in. If you become tolerant of something, then you will not desire any change. Therefore, you must become resolute in accepting change.

Try not to compare your season with others as you do not know what God is doing in someone else's life. Also, know that it is not our job to try and change God's timing (stepping out of His will to make things happen in our strength). It is our job to discern (recognize) it so that we can be in alignment with His will.

## COACH YOURSELF

When was the last time you accessed your season? Describe the season you believe you are in.

_____
_____
_____
_____
_____

What do you need to stop tolerating so your life can change?

_____
_____
_____
_____
_____

Have you ever felt like you stepped out of God's will? How was that experience for you?

_____

_____

_____

_____

What can you do to prepare for hard seasons?

_____

_____

_____

_____

### KEY LESSONS

- Remember, no season is permanent, but you need patience to endure.
- The key to accepting that a season has changed is to let go of fear.
- There is always a reason for a season, even if we cannot comprehend it.
- You cannot change what you tolerate, so if you are willing to tolerate it, then it will not change.

**"**

*Vision without action is merely a dream. Action without vision just passes the time. Vision with action can change the world.*

— *Joel A. Barker*

**"**

## Chapter 6

# Journal the Vision

*"Thus says the Lord, the God of Israel, 'Write all the words which I have spoken to you in a book.'" (Jeremiah 30:2 – ESV).*

I remember at nine years old my mother gave me a diary for my birthday. Maybe she realized I loved writing, or maybe it was a practical gift for a young girl, but whatever the reason, the habit of writing in a diary/journal began.

My journals before "salvation days" were something I am sure you would not want to read. I cringed when I read the things I wrote like my hide and go seek boys days, graphic sex scenes, bargaining moments with God, many heartbreaking experiences, and my obsession with Baby Cham (don't judge me). All I can say is, Jesus saves!

My newfound passion and desire to grow in deeper intimacy with God improved my unhealthy journaling habits.

After I recommitted my life to Christ in January 2014, I became even more intentional about discovering my purpose on this earth. I did this through various experiences such as learning about my gifts, sharing my story, pursuing my passions, attending Bible school, among others. I realized that the more I surrendered my plans and dreams to the Lord, the more He revealed Himself to me.

It was not until January 2016 when I decided to spend two days locked away with the Lord in worship, reading His Word and praying, that God started revealing more and more of His vision for my life. So I sat down and journaled all I discerned He was saying.

*If you don't know where you are going, you will not go anywhere.*

God speaks to us through various mediums, and He is always revealing His will for our lives, if we keep connected to Him. For me, I started to receive various prophecies from people of God everywhere I went, specifically about me impacting lives and ministering the gospel globally.

Deep down, I honestly knew I was meant for more, but I did not know what that "more" looked like. So, I kept thinking about getting more qualifications and looking into changing my career path as a way to fill that desire for more. My hunger and thirst for righteousness and to please God was growing; I prayed more, watched sermons, listen to worship music, and read godly books. It came to the point where I felt so stuck as to what my purpose truly was and what God's vision for my life really looked like.

While I kept receiving prophecies, I did not hold on to them because a part of me needed to hear from God myself. That did not happen until I decided to have more quiet time with Him and stopped being Miss Busy Body.

### GETTING GOD'S VISION FOR YOUR LIFE

Here are a few steps I took to realize God's vision for my life:

1. Surrender My Plans: Write down all the things you desire and see yourself doing. It means being honest to share with God even the BIG dreams you would not dare let anyone see and also the small desires you think He does not care about. This is not a one-time activity; it is as often as you can, sharing your heart with God through prayer and journaling.

2. Feeding and Exposing Myself to Great Possibilities: The truth is, my experiences were limited based on a lack of exposure growing up in the inner-city, but also the fact that I live in a Third World Country. Through the internet, I learnt about blogging (a way to use my writing gift) and attending conferences (going to Pinky Promise Conference in 2015). I saw things like retractable banners and women selling inspirational t-shirts, just to name a few. These gave me ideas of things I could do to enhance my first "She's Royal Conference."

So, you have to open your mind to learn new things and be humble yet diligent enough to act on the things you learn.

3. Receive God's Vision: Again, this means you want to spend time listening to God. Write down everything that comes to you in your quiet time, even when it does not make sense. When God revealed to me that I would own a publishing company, be a full-time entrepreneur, travel globally to speak, and write multiple books, none of these made any sense. Dream with God and become resolute in your heart that God's will is non-negotiable. Sometimes God does not reveal His plans because we have a mindset that we will not accept it if we do not like what we hear. So, when you sing that you surrender all to the Lord, ensure that you actually mean it.

4. Ask God Questions: In some denominations or Christian practices, people are taught to see God as a judge who wants to strike them down when they do something wrong. The Bible refers to God as a Father, a good one too (See Psalms 103:13). God refers to you as a friend, not a slave (See John 15:15). This means you are allowed to ask God questions about your future or anything else. The key is to trust that He is ordering your steps. So follow the leading of the Holy Spirit and write what you hear. If you feel unsure about something, ask Him for confirmations like Gideon. If it feels too impossible, ask Him for help like Moses. Again, just trust the Father's heart towards you.

*"My sheep hear My voice, and I know them, and they follow Me." (John 10:27 – KJV).*

5. Obey and take small faith steps on what God has already revealed to you. If you are sensing that God is saying you should go back to school, then start applying. If you are sensing that God is saying you should write a book, then start jotting down topics. If you are sensing that God is saying you should launch a ministry, then start evangelizing to people around you. Taking faith steps will build your confidence, plus you are showing God that you are willing to please Him by being obedient.

Do not get stuck on expecting God to reveal His vision to you exactly as He did for me or anyone else. For some people, God reveals His will through dreams, prophetic words, while you are reading the Word, by using what someone says to plant a seed in your heart, through a worship song, exercising, while driving, reading a book, and many other means.

God is sovereign, meaning that He has the power, wisdom, and authority to do anything He chooses when it comes to Him revealing His vision for your life. Just remain prayerful, grow in discernment, trust that the Holy Spirit is leading you, and continue developing an intimate relationship with Him. He is not trying to hide His vision or will for you.

## THREE PROMISES GOD HAS DECLARED ABOUT HIS VISION FOR YOUR LIFE

*Promise #1*
God will complete the work He has started in you. This means you can surrender your desires to God and trust that anything He instructs you to do is never to hurt you. While insecurities will say you are unqualified, keep your focus on the One who gave you the assignment because He will hold your hands through it.

"Being confident of this, that he who began a good work in you will carry it on to completion until the day of Christ Jesus." (Philippians 1:6 – NIV).

*Promise #2*
You will not have to accomplish God's vision alone. He says He will never leave you or forsake you (See Deuteronomy 31:8). There will be seasons when things feel unbearable, but as the songwriter says, "When you see one set of footprints in the sand, it is God carrying you through."

*"Be strong and courageous. Do not be afraid or terrified because of them, for the Lord your God goes with you; he will never leave you nor forsake you." (Deuteronomy 31:6 – NIV).*

*Promise #3*
God is the giver of good gifts. This idea that God will call you to do something you hate is a lie. Again, it will make us uncomfortable sometimes. It might stretch our faith, and you

might face a few obstacles (remember the enemy is here to kill, steal, and destroy (See John 10:10), but Jesus came so that you can live an abundant life and the blessings of the Lord will add no sorrow to you.

Discomfort does not have to lead to depression. If you remind yourself you are in God's will, then you will find joy even in discomfort because you know you are becoming more like Christ.

*"Every good and perfect gift is from above, coming down from the Father of the heavenly lights, who does not change like shifting shadows." (James 1:17- NIV).*

## POWER OF WRITING DOWN YOUR DREAMS

*"Journal writing gives us insights into who we are, who we were, and who we can become."*
– *Sandra Marinella*

Maybe you have been journaling for a while, or maybe you have not yet started. I want to close this chapter by sharing five benefits of journaling your visions or dreams.

1. It gives you a chance to release your emotions on paper so you will decrease stress, not bottling everything.

2. It propels you towards your goals and gives you a clearer vision for your life.

3. It boosts gratitude for life as you share more of your blessings and answered prayers on paper.

4. You are able to explore your thoughts and become more self-aware, especially if you have journaling prompts and reflection exercises.
5. It enhances your creativity and develops your "voice."

## COACH YOURSELF

What do you believe God has placed you on earth to do?

_____
_____
_____
_____
_____
_____


Close your eyes and dream about your life. What are some of the things you see yourself accomplishing or having?

_____
_____
_____
_____
_____
_____

What was your childhood dream, and why? What happened to that dream and why?

_____

_____

_____

_____

_____

What type of life do you really want to live?

_____

_____

_____

_____

_____

### KEY LESSONS

- Journaling allows you to keep a record of God's blessings in your life.
- Journaling is a two-part process: you speaking to God and writing it down, and you listening to God and writing it down.
- Create time to sit in God's presence so He can share His plans for your life.
- When God shares His vision for your life, it will motivate you in challenging times.

**"**

*Desire is the key to motivation, but it's determination and commitment to an unrelenting pursuit of your goal — a commitment to excellence — that will enable you to attain the success you seek"*

— *Mario Andretti*

**"**

Chapter 7

# Become ~~Self-~~ GOD -Motivated

*"So, then, brothers and sisters, don't let anyone move you off the foundation of your faith. Always excel in the work you do for the Lord. You know that the hard work you do for the Lord is not pointless." (1 Corinthians 15:58 – GOD'S WORD).*

### WHAT IS MOTIVATION?

According to Webster's Dictionary, motivation is a force or influence that causes someone to do something. It is the "why" that fuels us to achieve our goals and purpose in life.

So often, we are taught that we must be self-motivated to get the most out of life. I agree that motivation is a crucial element in getting the most out of life, but as believers, our motivation must be different from unbelievers. Our motivation should be inspired by God and our desire should be to do His will. Psalm 73:25 says, "Whom have I in heaven but you? And there is nothing on earth that I desire besides you." (NIV). Therefore, our desires should not be driven by the things of this world.

As believers, we are called to deny ourselves, take up the cross, and follow Christ (See Matthew 16:24). This is a dying of our selfish desires, but we are driven to please, obey, and follow Christ. If we are not motivated (driven to achieve, develop, and keep moving forward), then we will live a wasted, mediocre and purposeless life.

"Self-motivation" is acceptable to unbelievers, but if we are submitted to a greater giver (God) than "self," then we can do even more than we can imagine. Ephesians 3:20 says, "Now to him who by the power that is working within us is able to do far beyond all that we ask or think." (NET). This alternative is what I call "God-Motivation."

## WHAT DRIVES YOU?

Wanting to do something and being motivated to achieve it are two different things. When you are ready to quit something or keep procrastinating because of fear, motivation pushes you to start.

Firstly, you should understand that godly goals are motivated by love: love for Jesus and or love for other people. If you are motivated by peer pressure, guilt, greed, materialism, revenge, pride, or jealousy, you will experience only temporary fulfillment. Anything that is not set on the foundation of Christ will be shaken eventually. Remember, God is more interested in why we do what we do than what we actually do.

Before we get into the three ways of becoming God-motivated, let us do a short quiz to give you a better understanding of how motivated you are.

Tick the responses that apply to you:

a. I place maximum effort in achieving my goals, and I work hard even if I suffer a setback.
**Never☐   Sometimes ☐   Very Often☐**

b. I regularly set goals and objectives to achieve my vision.
**Never☐   Sometimes ☐   Very Often ☐**

c. I am enthused about my goals and never worry about achieving them because I know it will work out.
**Never☐   Sometimes ☐   Very Often ☐**

d. I always believe that if I work hard and trust God, I can accomplish great things.
**Never☐   Sometimes ☐   Very Often☐**

*If most of your responses were "never," you have been allowing your personal doubts and fears to keep you from succeeding. Now is the time to break this harmful pattern and start believing in your God-given goals again.*

*If most of your responses were "sometimes," you are doing okay on being God-motivated. To achieve your goals, try connecting more with your "why."*

*If most of your responses were "very often," Wonderful! You are getting things done. Continue inspiring others with your success.*

Let us begin working on becoming God-motivated.

## BE CONFIDENT

Being God-motivated is having confidence that you are able to accomplish your goals and purpose. You are confident that God has equipped you for the tasks ahead and this faith and unwavering trust in God propels you to remain resilient even when you face setbacks (See Psalm 31:24, Joshua 1:9). If you do not believe you are able to achieve it, then you are already defeated. This confidence is not found in our strengths and abilities but is from a God-assurance that He is always with us (See Philippians 4:13).

## SURROUND YOURSELF WITH GODLY AND MOTIVATED PEOPLE

There are many godly people, but not all of them are motivated. Many people sit in church with thoughts of lack and mediocrity. Such thoughts will not help you to become God-motivated. Your environment can make or break you, so you have to be intentional about the relationships that you engage in. Real friends bring out the best in each other. They encourage and motivate each other to achieve their goals. Know that you cannot achieve God's vision for your life by yourself, so you need others to help push you to be your best.

Romans 12:5 says, "In Christ we, though many, form one body, and each member belong to all others." (NIV).

## START BELIEVING IN THE POSSIBILITIES

"Everything is possible for one who believes." (Mark 9:23 – NIV).
Reread the verse above; did it say "some things?" No, everything is possible for you if you believe. As a believer, you should be one of the most creative and innovative persons because you serve a God who is full of endless possibilities. Too many believers are narrow-minded, and a lack of faith causes this.

Unbelief limits your life. The more you trust and believe in God, the more limitless your possibilities become. To become God-motivated, you have to become a faith-walker, faith-talker, and faith-thinker. Possibilities are only seen through faith. "Without faith it is impossible to please God." (Hebrews 11:6 – NIV). It is time for you to become a "possibility thinker." God wants to expand the possibilities in your life; you just have to trust Him.

We have looked at three ways to become God-motivated; however, this will not happen overnight. It will require sacrifice and focus from you. Your attitude and beliefs about achieving your goals and dreams are dependent on you. God has already given you so many promises to remind you that He is always with you. So, even when the obstacles arise, you can press on because God has already equipped you for the journey.

## COACH YOURSELF

Reflect on those moments when you thought you could not accomplish something. What made you go on?

_____
_____
_____
_____
_____

Evaluate your current "inner" circle. Are they encouragers or criticizers?

_____
_____
_____
_____

In what areas of your life are you limiting God through your unbelief?

_____
_____
_____
_____
_____

## KEY LESSONS

- Being God-motivated is having confidence that you are able to accomplish your goals and purpose.
- Wanting to do something and being motivated to achieve it are two different things.
- Motivation helps you to bounce back from setbacks on the success journey.
- Being God-motivated helps you to focus on your values and inspires you to please God.

"
*When you think you've surrendered, surrender some more."*
— *Gabby Bernstein*
"

# Chapter 8

# Be Still (Surrender)

*"My sheep hear my voice, and I know them, and they follow me:" (John 10:27 – ESV). .*

There is a constant desire to accomplish more things to fulfill us. Understand that nothing can ever truly make us happy or fulfilled because God made us with a space that only He can fill. How does God fill us? He fills us through stillness and surrender.

> **Stillness is very difficult in this culture that promotes achievement over integrity and busyness over quietness.**

It is in stillness that we enter into deeper intimacy with God. It allows us to hear God clearer, decrease distraction, and experience God's nearness. Stillness is very difficult in this culture that promotes achievement over integrity and busyness over quietness. Stillness is not about being unproductive; it is a posture of your heart that heightens your spiritual senses.

Three powerful results of being still before God include:

- You will come into alignment with God's will. Throughout the scriptures, you see Jesus spending time in His Father's presence, so He could hear from Him.

- In stillness you are replenished. Life can be so overwhelming with daily responsibilities and tasks that we end up pouring out while our mental, spiritual, and physical energy become depleted. It is in God's presence that you will be able to recharge.

- Stillness allows us to be able to get a better perspective and discern the season we are in.

*"The greatest blessing connected with stillness is that we can hear eternity; we can hear the voice of the Eternal One as He speaks to our conscience."*

— *O. Hallesby*

## A CALL TO SURRENDER

Many understand surrender in terms of accepting Jesus Christ as Savior; the challenge many struggle with is Jesus as Lord. As Lord, it means you are allowing Him free reign over your life, and this requires a constant dying to self.

Surrender is you demonstrating faith in God and His promises. It is a daily commitment to giving it all to God. Surrender is difficult for us because it means we have to give up our control; giving up control means we will have to be vulnerable.

Our minds are often so consumed about life, goals, relationships, money, or the future. True surrender comes from trusting God fully. It frees you to enjoy the faith journey and persevere through even the challenges of life. Surrender is you saying to God, "I want what You want because You know what's best."

How to get into the habit of being still and surrendering:

- Practice spending time daily in God's presence. You can do this by creating a routine quiet time where you set an appointment with God. Schedule time in your calendar to meet with the Lover of your Soul.

- Read, study, and ruminate on God's Word. God's Word is the foundation we build our lives on, so reading it is us drawing closer to God.

- Pray without ceasing. Maintain an active prayer time where you are sharing your thoughts with God and listening to Him. Ask God to calm your mind.

- Develop a lifestyle of worship. This includes reflecting on God's goodness, singing songs of praises, praying thanksgiving prayers, and pouring your heart out to Him.

- Journal your thoughts, prayers, dreams, and concerns to God. Pour out your concerns, visualize your goals, and express constant gratitude.

- Take your thoughts captive and make them subject to Christ. Our thoughts seem to go a mile per minute, and so often, it leads to distraction. Philippians 4:8 challenges us to think on pure, lovely, praiseworthy, true, and admirable thoughts.

- Have a place designated to meet Him often. Find a space where you feel peace and quietness where there is no disturbance to go pour your heart out to the Lord.

- Maintain relationships and fellowship with other believers who you can trust to pray with and for you, and you can do the same. Sometimes life gets so overwhelming that you struggle to pray for yourself but find people who can intercede for you.

- Exchange your will for God's will. This comes through praying, discerning, trusting, listening, and having faith to take action on what God says. Sometimes God's will may not seem to be what we initially desire, but it is for this reason you need to grow to trust Him more and believe His promises that He knows what is best for you.

So often we talk about the cost of surrender and focus on all the things we give up; but I want you to know that surrender is an investment. An investment is giving up something with expectations of a greater return.

When you surrender to God, you will get a return (one that exceeds what you have given up). You should know God has the best gifts, best plans, and a far better future in store than you could even imagine. So, whatever you surrender (no matter how valuable it feels at the time), God has better in store. This mindset shift is so important for you to truly overcome your insecurities. In your stillness, your discernment heightens, your faith grows, you become more courageous and your impact will be greater. That is what surrender does: ALIGNS you for better.

## COACH YOURSELF

What plan(s) are you creating and seeking God for?

_____

_____

_____

_____

_____

_____

_____

Describe your daily quiet time. How can you improve it?

_____
_____
_____
_____
_____

Who can you connect with to be a prayer and accountability partner to support this faith walk?

_____
_____
_____
_____
_____
_____

Journal a prayer of surrender to the Lord, to exchange your will for His will.

_____
_____
_____
_____
_____

**KEY LESSONS**

- In stillness, we get into alignment.
- Surrender leads to joy, peace, and true fulfillment.
- Surrender involves obedience to God's Word, God's plans, and walking in God's will.
- If you do not love God's Word, then you do not love God. True love to the Lord is demonstrated through obedience, commitment, and surrender.

> *Smiles and tears are so alike with me; they are neither of them confined to any particular feelings: I often cry when I am happy, and smile when I am sad.*
>
> — *Anne Brontë*

Chapter 9

## Crying Is Allowed

*"... Weeping may last through the night, but joy comes with the morning." (Proverbs 30:5 – NIV).*

Writing a chapter entitled "Crying is Allowed" must be from God because I am a rough girl. I have been described as being emotionally constipated by exes (cover eyes) because I use to pride myself on not showing emotions since it made me look weak. This journey with Christ has challenged a lot of my crazy beliefs; the idea that crying makes you soft or weak is based on societal norms and is not true. It actually takes a woman of strength to accept her emotions without being led by them.

I have had some really on the cloud moments where God showed up and showed out with blessings overflowing in my life. I have also had some moments of crying (no bawling). Good crying with tears of joy and bad crying with heartbreaks I did not think I could recover from.

It is very important to share your emotions with God. Through His Holy Spirit, even God Himself shows emotions, such as grieving (See Ephesians 4:30).

Casting all your care upon him; for he careth for you. (1 Peter 5:7 - KJV).

Our emotions are part of us, and God is concerned about our entire being. He only asks us not to be led by our emotions but to instead be led by His Spirit. God can handle whatever emotional experience you may have on your faith journey.

Again, when I say crying is allowed, I mean happy tears, sad tears, angry tears, or even worry tears. God wants us to cast our cares on Him because He truly cares.

Most of our insecurities come from various experiences, especially the negative and most painful ones. In those moments, many of us as women build up walls to protect us without processing our emotions. When emotions are suppressed for long period of time, you find that you struggle to move on from certain traumas/experiences.

Undealt with emotions affects your ability to:

- talk about things that matter to you.
- build healthy friendships and intimate relationships.
- empathize with others.
- encourage or praise yourself.

- You may find yourself going along with situations instead of expressing what you really want and need.
- Use various activities to help you numb and avoid feelings you do not want to explore.
- spend most of your time with other people to avoid being alone.
- show passive-aggressive behaviors to deal with situations that upset you.

It is important to get more comfortable with your emotions, even the ones that do not feel great. It will help you navigate the challenges of life more successfully while also improving your relationship with God, yourself, and anyone else you care about.

Here are a few benefits of crying:

- *Crying helps to soothe us, calm us, and relieve us when we are in distress.*

- *Crying improves our mood. Have you ever cried about something and felt better after? I am sure you have had this experience.*

- *Did you know that crying can lower your blood pressure and reduce toxins in your body?*

Crying is one way to connect with your emotions. You do not need to feel embarrassed about being human.

### Dear Insecurity

Many brave persons in scripture cried, including David, Jacob, Joseph, Hezekiah, Ezra, Mordecai, Peter, and even Jesus. Be comforted that tears are a language that God understands, and crying means you are in good company.

## COACH YOURSELF

When you think about total surrender to God, what fears come up?

_____

_____

_____

Write three things you are thankful for.

_____

_____

_____

What area of your life are you most unhappy with and why? (Friends, career, relationships, finances)

_____

_____

_____

_____

_____

Share an experience where you cried tears of joy.

_____
_____
_____
_____

### KEY LESSONS

- Your emotions matter to God.
- Even Jesus wept; why feel bad if you do.
- Crying can be a sign of surrender from relying on yourself and giving it to God.
- Crying does not mean you are weak; it means you have a heart.

**"**

*There is no passion to be found playing small--in settling for a life that is less than the one you are capable of living."*
— *Nelson Mandela*

**"**

Chapter 10

# Pursue Your Passions

*"Lead a life worthy of your calling, for you have been called by God." (Ephesians 4:1 – NLT).*

Passion is a powerful emotion that energizes and motivates us. It is what fires us up and gives our lives meaning. Without a pursuit of your passion, you will find your life dull and less fulfilling because passion gives us great satisfaction.

For many persons, they had big dreams when they were younger, but with life's trials and the many obstacles they have faced, they abandoned these dreams.

I believe God gave us a passion for personal satisfaction and ensuring that we bring Him glory.

We have been cultured to believe that our job or career should be something we do not like, and we should consider it as a means to survive. So many people stay stuck in jobs they hate, living life aimlessly and passionlessly.

To overcome your insecurities, you have to believe that God do not desire you to settle in anything or anywhere that you are not passionate about. Your career or job does not have to be something you hate and wake up daily feeling like a drag. You can discover your passion and pursue it.

Your passion will keep you going in the hard moments because it brings so much joy and purpose.

*"Find what you are passionate about and it will lead to your life purpose."*
*— Carla R. Cannon*

## STORY TIME

I always knew I wanted to help people from I was young. Growing up in the inner city, I really desired to mentor teen girls because it really bothered me that so many of them were settling or wasting their lives. So I became very involved in community youth clubs and took up leadership roles so I could serve other young people.

In 2009, I entered the Festival Queen competition, of course, because it was a dream of mine but mainly because the winner would get funding to do a community project. This was my opportunity to launch my mentorship program in my community. I did not win, but the passion for helping the young ladies kept growing. So, I wrote a plan to host a summer program for teen girls.

I was nineteen years old and working a full-time job, attending university for my bachelor's degree, and at the time, I was still living in the inner-city, sleeping on the ground in the boardhouse with my parents. I sent letters to business persons in the community to sponsor meals; sent letters to churches to use their building as the venue, designed and printed flyers and application forms, then walked all around the Kencot community inviting young ladies to this one-week workshop and mentorship program.

I did not get a lot of sponsorship, but I got a few so I saved my salary to help. I took my vacation for the week and got speakers to come and share with the ladies. My mother also took her vacation that week to cook lunch for the girls. My mother always believed in me and supported me in all my endeavors; God bless her heart so much. Approximately twenty-two young ladies attended. We had activities for them, and on the last day, we gave awards for various areas, for example, best behavior, most improved, among others.

I did various versions of mentoring teen girls through events where only five girls showed up. I was faithful in little because numbers never mattered; it was always about the impact.

Fast forward to the summer of 2020 when COVID hit. I was led to do the teen girls mentorship program online and five hundred teens from countries all over the world registered

(Haiti, Trinidad, Nigeria, Ghana, Dominica, Jamaica, Florida, New York, St. Lucia and more), which birthed my newest ministry "Empowering Girls Club."

I shared this story to show that if you truly desire to pursue your passion, you do not need permission from anyone, you do not need loads of money, and you do not need a big platform. It starts with a desire, put together a plan, take actions by faith, and just start whatever it is.

My life has never felt unfulfilling or boring. I have many passions, and I try to go after them. Some might not turn out the way I intended, but it is okay because life is better when you know you tried than to live a life wondering "What if."

Whatever you feel passionate about, go after it; try something today. So many possibilities exist with the internet, and you will not regret trying. Sometimes you do not have to start something new as there are so many organizations that are looking for volunteers, and you can start there.

Your passion should be bigger than you and not just about personal achievements. It is an ability to serve others, give back, and have a major impact.

If you do not know what you are passionate about, ask yourself what gives you joy? What problem in the world would you love to solve? What breaks your heart that you wish you could do something about?

I will add too that you can discover your passion and build a business or find a career that allows you to use your gifts, skills, and talents even in your professional life. There are endless possibilities that exist now.

By pursuing your passion, you will also build your character. It takes true courage to go after what you truly desire in life.

I believe in you, and God believes in you. Go after all God has for you.

## COACH YOURSELF

What is one thing you do easily with the least amount of effort?

_____
_____
_____
_____
_____

If you were financially secure, what would you do with your time?

_____
_____
_____
_____

Dear Insecurity

How do you want to be remembered fifty years from now?

_____
_____
_____
_____

What do you genuinely feel passionate about?

_____
_____
_____
_____

### KEY LESSONS

- Passion is the energy that keeps us going and fills us with excitement.
- Passion includes doing work that you love, and it allows you to make an impact.
- When you follow your passion in life, your dreams manifest into reality.
- When you follow your passion in life and do what you love for a living, it will not feel like work.

**"**

*Trusting God is not a one-time fix. LIFE will always happen to you but you have a choice to make. You can either depend on your situation or depend on Christ.*

— *Heather Lindsey*

**"**

# Chapter 11

# Trust The Process

*"Trust in the Lord with all your heart and lean not on your own understanding, in all your ways acknowledge Him and He will direct your paths" (Proverbs 3:5-6 – MEV).*

Certainly, we all wish that life was filled with mostly happy days, and when we pray, all our prayers are answered. Can you imagine!

The truth is, this life on earth is a test, as Rick Warren says. It means sometimes things will be good and we will have the best time of our lives, but there will be other times when nothing seems to make sense.

Here is what we must learn to do – *Trust the Process.* This means that sometimes, or most times, we will not understand why things happen, and we will not have control, but we serve a God who we can trust to work things together for our good (See Romans 8:28).

We trust God because:

- He knows ALL things.
- Everything is possible with Him.
- He sees the end from the beginning.
- He always has your best interest at heart.
- Nothing comes as a surprise to Him.
- He is faithful and good.
- His Word cannot return to Him void, so whatever He promises you, He will fulfill.

We trust the process because we trust God, and we do not rely on ourselves. We can fail at things, but God does not fail.

Do not allow your self-worth to be attached to an outcome or your failure to achieve something. It can result in feelings of pain and suffering. Failing does not define who you are.

Trusting the process is a part of the faith journey. It will save you unnecessary worry to be perfect and to be afraid of failing or becoming self-reliant. It also makes waiting on God's timing more bearable.

## COACH YOURSELF

What is one area of your life where you are waiting on God to show up? Is it hard to wait patiently, and why?

_____

_____

What can you do to remind yourself to wait patiently on God's timing?

Share your personal experience of trusting God in an area of your life.

Why do you think you struggle with trusting the process sometimes?

## KEY LESSONS

- Trusting God requires faith and perseverance.
- Sometimes waiting on God is about trusting in His timing, and other times, it is about acting on what He has already told you.
- During the "process," your character grows, your faith is strengthened, and your discernment heightens.
- Trusting the process means you know and have faith that God has a divine plan for your life and He will fulfill His promise.

"

*Faith is to believe what you do not see; the reward of this faith is to see what you believe.*
— *Saint Augustine*

"

Chapter 12

## Level-Up Your Faith

*"And He said to them, "Because of the littleness of your faith; for truly I say to you, if you have faith the size of a mustard seed, you will say to this mountain, 'Move from here to there,' and it will move; and nothing will be impossible to you." (Matthew 17:20 – NASB).*

Faith is considered as "belief, not proof." It is an assurance of something that is going to happen even before it has. Many people struggle with faith because the average person has to see something before they believe that it exists.

Faith is the currency for living a purposeful and impactful life in God's economy. It is a confident assurance that whatever God says, it is so, even though physically, it has not yet manifested. Faith is a gift from God that was planted in us. That seed of faith grows when we take action toward what we believe. It is through your faith that you truly please God and you are able to overcome doubt, fear and anxiety.

"Leveling up" (growing) in faith is crucial to the immeasurable success and abundance you can achieve. Yes, we can have some level of success, doing things logically but whatever you achieve in your own strength or wisdom pales in comparison to what God can and will do in you.

Faith operates in the realm of the invisible. It is for this reason the power of visualization has impacted so many people; they see what God says long before they receive it tangibly.

Insecurity is heightened when we operate in fear or allow fear to doubt God. However, if we increase our trust, reliance, and belief in God, then our faith also increases. We prove our faith by taking action.

*"Resist your fear; fear will never lead you to a positive end. Go for your faith and what you believe."*
— *T.D Jakes*

You build your faith when you hear God's Word repeatedly and not just once in a while. When you read God's Word out loud, you will learn that God's Word coming out of your mouth has the power to transform you from the inside out. Why? Faith comes by hearing and hearing by the Word of God. (See Romans 10:17).

If your knowledge of God is limited, then your faith will be limited. So, your faith will grow as you take deliberate steps toward your goals.

Remember, your faith is in God, not the world system or strategies. You know you are operating in faith when the vision of living life in purpose, impact, and abundance is bigger than you are.

*"Look at the proud! They trust in themselves, and their lives are crooked. But the righteous will live by their faithfulness to God." (Habakkuk 2:4 – NLT).*

Therefore, level-up your faith so you can start accessing God's promises. You can do that by:

- Growing in deeper intimacy with God so you can know His voice and obey when He speaks.

- Being willing to take action (show your faith by your works).

- Declare God's promises and affirm His Word daily.

### COACH YOURSELF

In what way(s) is God prompting you to step out by faith in this season?

_____

_____

_____

_____

"With God all things are possible" (See Matthew 19:26). What does this verse mean to you?

What can you start doing to "level up" your faith?

I really want God to…

## KEY LESSONS

- Wherever you place your focus, is where you will experience abundance.
- Faith is believing, even when you do not know how it will happen.
- When you have faith in your dreams, goals and the plans God has for you, you cannot be easily distracted.
- Faith enables you to overcome every obstacle in your path toward success.
- Without faith and belief in your calling, you will not be able to live the purposeful and impactful life God has for you.

"

*I believe that God has put gifts and talents and ability on the inside of every one of us. When you develop that and you believe in yourself and you believe that you're a person of influence and a person of purpose, I believe you can rise up out of any situation.*

— *Joel Osteen*

"

## Chapter 13

# Discover Your Gifts

*"Each one, as a good manager of God's different gifts, must use for the good of others the special gift he has received from God." (1 Peter 4:10 – GNT).*

Each of us was given innate abilities and natural talents. Sometimes, it is hard to explain the difference between gifts and talents, but from a biblical perspective, we are taught about spiritual gifts given by God when we get saved. God gives both natural talents and spiritual gifts.

Talents are a bit easier to recognize, especially if they are cultivated from a young age. Consider Michael Jordan with basketball, Usain Bolt with track and field, Tasha Cobbs with singing, and many others. Even now, you can probably picture growing up and easily remembering the children who stood out because they seemed to be more talented.

As you grew older, if you were not cultivating these talents, then life happened, and we instead focused on career. Discovering gifts were not always at the forefront of our mind.

Most times, people get to a point where the question of "What is my purpose" starts to bother them. It is in this season of desiring to do more and be more that the question of "What am I gifted at or what am I passionate about" begins to matter.

God has a purpose for your life, and your gifts were given to you to do what He asks of you. God will never ask you to do something that He does not give you the ability to do.

Everyone has a gift. Certainly, there are people with more gifts than others, but no matter how many gifts you have been given, God has given you these gifts to impact others. It is crucial for you to be aware of your gifts because it brings true fulfillment to life when you use them.

Which of these statements describes you?

a) I do not believe I have any gifts.
b) I know deep down I possess gifts, but I just do not know what they are.
c) I know my gifts, and I have been using them, but I know there is room for more.

Sometimes our gifts are not easily identified and require soul searching. The gift(s) may have been locked away by past traumas or pain and is waiting for the chance to shine.

## IDENTIFY YOUR SPIRITUAL GIFTS

Discovering your God-given spiritual gifts allows you to experience maximum fulfillment in your life with minimum frustration. There is more to your Christian life than just accepting the gift of salvation. That is crucial, but you are also called and equipped to fulfill God's purpose, and using your spiritual gifts is a part of that. So, exercising your spiritual gifting is a vital and exciting part of your spiritual journey.

*"There are different kinds of gifts, but the same Spirit distributes them. There are different kinds of service, but the same Lord." (1 Corinthians 12:4 - NIV).*

The Holy Spirit gives you spiritual gifts to build up God's kingdom and edify the church. There is a lot of confusion around some gifts that are seemingly "celebrated" by the church. However, do not get caught up in popularity because EVERY single spiritual gift is important to God, and your contribution is also important.

One of my gifts is to help others to identify their gifts and equip them to understand how they can use them to impact others. In this book, I really want you to become more aware of your gifts so you can experience the fullness of who God has called you to be.

Many people ask how many spiritual gifts are there and some say twelve major gifts, but you will see far more listed in the scriptures. Read 1 Corinthians 12:8-10, 1 Corinthians 12:28, Romans 12:6-8, Ephesian 4:11 and 1 Timothy 2:1-2.

Theologians have broken down the main gifts into three categories: Ministry, Manifestation, and Motivation. As you read through this list, you may be able to identify a few gifts that are more evident in your life, or it might awaken a desire in you to learn even more about your gifts.

### MINISTRY GIFTS

**Apostleship:** overseeing and leading a ministry or missionary effort.

**Evangelism:** the ability to successfully communicate the message of the gospel, especially to nonbelievers.

**Pastor/Shepherd:** nurture, care for, and guide people in their spiritual journey.

**Teaching:** understanding and explaining biblical truth to help others apply it to their lives and grow in faith.

### MANIFESTATION GIFTS

**Faith:** having confidence in God that He will provide, protect, and answer prayers.

**Healing:** using your ability to pray, touch, or speak words that produce spiritual, physical, or emotional healing.

**Words of Wisdom:** the ability to apply spiritual truth to meet specific needs or situation.

**Words of Knowledge:** to provide truth by revealing critical information, biblical understanding, or supernatural insight.

**Miracles:** showing God's power through supernatural action.

**Discernment:** having special ability to tell right from wrong or truth from deception.

**Tongues:** talking in a language unknown to the speaker for the purpose of prayer, worship, or for edifying others.

**Interpretation of Tongues:** telling others what someone said in tongues.

## MOTIVATION GIFTS

**Mercy:** providing compassion to the poor and hurting.

**Leadership:** having vision, motivating, and building teams to advance God's kingdom.

**Prophecy:** the ability to speak truth and/or future information. This gift edifies, corrects, and comforts.

**Giving:** generously provide money and resources for ministry.

**Serving:** assisting a ministry or person in meeting needs and accomplishing objectives.

**Exhortation:** encouraging people through words of comfort and inspiration.

**Administration:** the ability to help steer the church, or a ministry, toward the successful completion of God-given goals, with skills in planning, organization, and supervision.

## OTHER SPIRITUAL GIFTS

**Hospitality**: offer food, housing, or relationship to provide a comfortable environment (See 1 Peter 4:9-10).

**Craftsmanship**: creativity to design or build items for ministry (See Exodus 31:3).

**Intercession**: pray for others in response to the Holy Spirit's prompting (See 1 Timothy 2:1-2).

Again, NO gift is better than another gift. EVERY gift has a purpose and was given to you by God to bless others.

*"So you should earnestly desire the most helpful gifts. But now let me show you a way of life that is best of all." (1 Corinthians 12:31 – NLT).*

Using your spiritual gifts is great, but it is more important to know how to love others. God has given you His love as a gift, so we should always extend this gift. You love because God loved you first. Without love, all the actions supposing to be gifts are empty.

Here are five spiritual gift examples of how you can practically serve others in the body:

1. **Gift of Serving/Helping:** singing on the choir, cooking or serving meals, decorating for special occasions, being an usher, being a greeter, being a host, being an A/V technician, driving church members to or from worship, using your personal skills as needed at church (painting, carpentry, plumber, electrician, mechanic, to name a few), maintaining the church grounds, and so on.

2. **Gift of Mercy:** joining the church care team (visiting homes, hospitals, nursing homes), serving funeral meals, working with single mothers, elderly or those going through difficulties, showing compassion for persons grieving, addicts, the abused, and others.

3. **Gift of Administration:** working alongside a church staff member, helping to coordinate administrative tasks, coordinating behind-the-scenes at concerts, volunteering as director of Vacation Bible School or other church programs, overseeing an area of ministry as an unpaid servant or chairing a committee, among other tasks.

4. **Gift of Teaching:** being a small group leader, adult class teacher, hosting Vacation Bible School, leading a Bible study, writing curriculum or training materials, and creating Bible lessons.

5. **Gift of Hospitality:** become a Sunday morning greeter, usher, parking lot attendant, host, preparing and serving

coffee at Sunday worship, helping plan church social events, arrange or provide housing for visiting missionaries, be a foster parent, arranging temporary housing needs for people in need, opening your home for Bible studies, small groups, youth activities (not necessarily leading any of them, just providing space).

I want to share how I have been using a few of my spiritual gifts to bring glory to God:

- **My gift of Faith:** with this gift, I have a trust and confidence in God that allows me to live boldly for Him and manifest that faith in mighty ways. Hosting a conference in 2015 without any money, believing God would provide for the two days, and having over one hundred women being blessed by God is an example of my gift in operation. Another example is leaving my comfortable nine to five job to pursue God's purpose as a Kingdom entrepreneur.

- **My gifts of Exhortation and Teaching:** the gift of exhortation (encouragement) can uplift and motivate others as well as challenge and rebuke them in order to foster spiritual growth and action. I do this as a speaker, coupled with my teaching gift. Also, professionally as a Christian Life Coach and Mentor, I use this gift to empower women from all over the world.

I hope you will start to think about how you too can bless others with your spiritual gifts.

## HONE YOUR NATURAL GIFTS/TALENTS

Your natural gifts and talents are those distinct, genetically inherited abilities you were born with. We all know people who are great at singing, dancing, leading, cooking, track and field, playing soccer, musical instruments, just to name a few.

It is normally something you are passionate about, you do without effort, and others also compliment you on. Think about your strengths and interests; these are all a part of your natural gifts.

Do not overthink and do not underplay yourself; be sensitive to God's leading in even using the things that come naturally to you.

## HOW TO ACTIVATE YOUR GIFTS FOR IMPACT

Here are some tips for discovering and stewarding your gifts:

1. **Start with prayer:** since God made you and placed these gifts in you, it means that He can reveal to you all the gifts He has blessed you with.

2. **Do a spiritual gifts test:** they are available online, and they tend to give you a good idea of what your gifts could be.

3. Reflect on the things you do naturally and enjoy doing. Think about what you enjoyed doing as a child; the

things you were drawn to as a teen, and the things you get lost in doing as an adult.

4. Ask persons around you what they think you are good at. Many times, people around you can see things in you that you never thought you were capable of.

5. After you have discovered your gifts, you want to start practicing to use them to serve others. It takes faith to step out and start using your gifts.

6. Do not compare your gifts with others. What God has called you to do is unique, so keep focused on becoming who God has called you to be.

7. Develop your gifts by practicing, studying to enhance them, and learning from others with similar abilities.

8. Exercise your faith by looking for opportunities to serve, lead, intercede, and motivate others. You do not need permission from "man" to do what God has already equipped you to do. I am not saying your church leaders are not important or you should not submit yourself to be guided by others, but so often we wait for a special occasion to share our gift with others. Example: you can use your gift of teaching to start a YouTube channel; you can use your gift of mercy or help to volunteer at an elderly's home; you can use your natural gift of playing the piano to serve on the praise team or offer piano lessons to children at church, or you

can use your gift of giving to sow money in the life of someone who needs help going back to school.

9. Allow your spiritual leaders to lay hands on you when you are going to use your gifts to minister publicly to others. It is a great encouragement to know you are being blessed by God's people for affirmation and support.

10. Believe God will use your gifts to make an impact in the world.

## COACH YOURSELF

How can you use your talents/passion to serve others?

_____
_____
_____
_____

What do people compliment you on the most? (Ask persons close to you what they think you are good at).

_____
_____
_____
_____

**Dear Insecurity**

What are some of the gifts you believe God has blessed you with that can serve others?

_____
_____
_____
_____

What are you doing to fulfill what you believe God has called you to do?

_____
_____
_____
_____

### KEY LESSONS

- Your gift is sometimes so deeply-rooted and natural that you do not recognize it.
- Never doubt what and how God can use your gifts to impact others.
- It offends God when you do not use the gift(s) He gave you.
- Knowing and operating in your gifts will give you true fulfillment and abundance.

**"**

*An unintentional life accepts everything and does nothing. An intentional life embraces only the things that will add to the mission of significance.*

*— John C Maxwell*

**"**

Chapter 14

# Be Bold. Be Extra. Be Intentional

*"God chose the foolish things of this world to shame the wise, and therefore let the one who boasts boast in the Lord." (1 Corinthians 1:27,31 – NIV).*

Do you believe you are capable of much more than you are presently doing, thinking, dreaming, or being? I think you are. How do I know? I know because you would not be reading this book.

That is the essence of potential; unexposed abilities, capped capabilities, hidden talents, and dormant power.

This is what this chapter is about: challenging you to tap into your potential.

Would you believe me if I told you that the same energy that you put into being lazy, procrastinating about your goals, settling for less than God's best and being ordinary, is the same energy that it takes to boldly go after your goals, be intentional about your success and accept that you were made to be extraordinary?

For many years, I heard that I talked too much, and while growing up, my closest friends used to say that I acted as if I knew too much. I heard it so often that I was just "too much." The more I heard this, the more I believed it; the more I believed it, the more I became comfortable and accepted mediocrity.

How did I know it was a mediocre life? Deep down, I knew I was made for more. I knew I had more to offer the world. I knew that there were passions I had that I buried so I would not be considered "too much."

Everything in your life is formed from habits, choices, and the words you speak.

Your habits are the actions you take daily. Your choices are the decisions you make daily. Your words are the things you declare over yourself daily, and these are the things that either hone or diminish your greatness.

## STORY TIME

As I have shared before, I grew up in the "ghetto," as many would say, in communities considered to be violence-prone and poverty-stricken. The yard I grew up in had many families; all of us with the same economic situation.

Today, when I look at my siblings and me and compare us to the persons we grew up with, our lives are drastically different. This was because we CHOSE to do and be different from what we saw around us. Many of the young men are now criminals, and some of the young ladies went into prostitution or settled for minimum wage jobs.

While I am sure that the fact that my father instilled the value of education in his children played a major role in the opportunities we were presented with, I still believe it came down to our CHOICES.

So, I want you to really pause and think about your life now.

*How often did you choose not to go after something you really wanted because you did not feel you deserved it?*

*How often have you accepted the negativity that others spoke over you as your reality?*

*How often did you do something out of your character because you wanted to fit in, and even after you did what they wanted you to do, you still felt like an outcast?*

*How often have you downplayed your dreams because you felt like you would "show up" others if you actually achieved them?*

Listen, you did not settle for ordinary because you are trying to "help" others. You settled because you are selfish. You are selfish because your potential was given to you by God to benefit others.

You only help, impact, or inspire others by being the best you that you are called to be and use the gifts you were born with to serve others. So, every time you choose timidity, you are robbing God of the glory He deserves.

Now, it is okay if, in the past, you refused to be bold and intentionally downplayed your gifts, desires, or dreams. You probably did not have anyone challenge you to be or do better; or you probably thought you had done all the right things and you are comfortable where you are at. Sorry, my friend, but God desires more from you. He has invested too much in you, and He is a God who desires returns on His investments (See Matthew 25:14-39).

You are reading this today because God is making a demand on you. God believes in you, and for that reason, He is challenging you not to settle anymore.

So, how do you become bold, become intentional, and become extraordinary? Kill your ego. Humble yourself. Surrender.

Your journey has little to do with you and more to do with others who will be better because you came across their path. Your insecurities do not just show up when you doubt yourself, they show up when you think you already have it together. That is pride, and that is saying you know more than God.

The closer you get to excellence in your life, the more friends you will lose. You have to accept that sometimes friendships are seasonal, and anything that does not align with the next level in Christ is not worth holding on to. People will love you when you are average because it also gives them permission to be comfortable. When you decide to pursue purpose and walk in your greatness, it will make people uncomfortable because they too know deep down that they were born for more.

Be encouraged that if you lose some people on your faith journey, God will align you with some genuine people who will cheer you on, so even a loss will work together for your good, if you love God.

Remember, purpose is found in being in God's will, and it is not His will for you to settle or stay in your comfort zone.

### COACH YOURSELF

Name one area in your life that you know you have settled for less than God's best and why?

_____
_____
_____
_____
_____
_____

**Dear Insecurity**

Who are you willing to become at the risk of walking boldly in your purpose?

_____
_____
_____
_____
_____

What are you willing to let go of so you can receive the greater that God has for you?

_____
_____
_____
_____
_____

What habits do you need to become intentional about developing so you can tap into your potential?

_____
_____
_____
_____
_____

## KEY LESSONS

- Settling for less is a sin if you are ignoring God's direction.
- Being ordinary is easier, so many remain on that path of mediocrity.
- Being extraordinary is you choosing daily to tap into your strengths, utilize your gifts, and explore your abilities.
- Stop dimming your light, refuse to speak negatively about yourself, and get out of your comfort zone; that is not God's will for your life.

Chapter 15

# Becoming The Woman God Has Called You To Be

I was very intentional in writing this book as a guide with simple yet practical and powerful steps to help you release self-doubt around who God has called you to be, so you can boldly activate your gifts to impact others.

As mentioned numerous times throughout the book, insecurity is not something you can snap your fingers and it disappears. It will require you to go over the chapters in this book a few times; some steps will be easier than others, but these principles are Spirit-led and, if taken, can truly transform your life as mine has been.

The world, the culture, and even Satan himself DO NOT want you to become the woman God has called you to be. I know many of your beliefs and behaviors have been years and years of seeds planted, but they can be uprooted in Jesus' name.

### Dear Insecurity

Being told by many that I would never amount to anything good, being labeled as "bad" girl, experiencing molestation, being told I talk too much by my closest friends, teachers, etc., being teased as "grater face, gremlin" because of my acne as a teenager, choosing to be the other woman for over seven years in a relationship because I did not believe I was worthy to be a man's first choice, doing two abortions, having my best friend malice me because I graduated top girl at high school, being a single mother from my child was born, getting pregnant in church, having to do a DNA test for my daughter, being robbed by my friend and her husband who I was a bridesmaid in their wedding, having clients attack me, etc. are just a few of the many experiences that led me to become insecure and believing I was not good enough to be used by God.

I am writing this book because I want you to know that nothing has disqualified you from God's plans, purpose, and destiny. You have to be willing to renew your mind from the things of the world. It is initially scary to go against the norms, but only those who are brave enough to say goodbye to insecurity can say hello to impact.

If you are ready to really become the woman God has called you to be, stop blaming everyone else (even if you feel you have the right to do so). When you take responsibility for your actions and reactions, then you will be healed and made whole to be different and do differently.

So I want to introduce you to five women. At one point, we have all been like one of these women or all of these women:

1. **Jealous Jane:** Do you find that you are genuinely happy for others? Are you someone who tends to diminish other's accomplishments? Do you find that you are always trying to prove you are better than others? Do you give others bad advice sometimes because you do not want them to do better than you? Let us be real: we ALL as women have struggled with feeling jealous over someone. Many times, listening to someone talk about their achievements can trigger our insecurities and remind us of our own inadequacies.

2. **Pity-Me Paula:** This is you if you are always blaming everyone for where you are at. Self-pity shows itself by you always feeling depressed, seeking validation for others, feeling you have no potential, your life is boring and mundane, everything feels like a struggle, you are afraid to be happy because you tell yourself bad things will always happen to you, no one likes to be around you, or you complain and nag others about your unfulfilled life.

3. **Lazy Lori:** You are a constant procrastinator, always starting but never finishing, run from challenges and desire everything to come easy, spend too much time watching TV or scrolling social media, wishing for things without working for it, you have no expectations, you are filled with excuses, you do not set goals or dream, or you set goals but year after year accomplish none.

4. **Doubtful Del:** You constantly compare yourself with others, you dismiss your gifts and talents, you are always preparing to defend yourself, you are always questioning if you are deserving or worthy, always second-guessing yourself, seeking validation from others, apologizing for success or failure, self-critical, afraid to make a decision, double-minded with your choices, worried about other's judgments or criticism, underplaying yourself, afraid to speak up or lead, or live in guilt from past choices.

5. **Criticizer Carla:** This can be two-fold – you are too self-critical or you are hypercritical (always finding faults with others). Some ways this shows up: you set impossibly high standards, afraid to task risks, worry a lot, struggle with anxiety over the future, always analyzing your mistakes, do not forgive easily, very harsh and moody towards others (especially when they do not live up to your expectations), bad-mouth others a lot behind their backs, discrediting others success, easily defensive, or afraid to give or receive compliments.

WOW, a lot, right!

Even writing this, I see myself in all these women at one point or another, but we do not want to be these women. Instead, we want to be like these other five women:

1. **Cheerleader Cami:** Always celebrating others' success, give compliments, share constructive criticism to help others grow, accept compliments, celebrate your wins, practice daily gratitude, give without expecting; people love being around you because you are always motivating others.

2. **Intercessor Iris:** Everyone loves a praying woman. Someone who goes to God not just for herself but on behalf of others. You "prophecy" and speak positive and godly words over others and over yourself. You value others and appreciate them for who God has called them to be, even if they do not see it for themselves yet.

3. **Bold Barbara:** You take responsibility for your reactions even when other's actions may be negative, you own your flaws, but you do not deal on them because you focus on who God made you to be; you acknowledge your strengths and use your gifts to bless others, you speak up for others and yourself, you celebrate small or big wins for yourself and others, you know your worth and do not settle for less than God's best, you try to be optimistic and be there for others.

4. **Faithful Fiona:** You are a good steward of the gifts God has given you; you try to be honest and authentic, you invest in others, you selflessly serve others, you are confident in who God made you to be, humble yet fearless, forgiving, and bearing the fruit of the Spirit.

5. **Extraordinary Erica:** Accepting that you have a purpose and your gift is bigger than you, you are not afraid to be the best version of yourself, motivated, consistent, always improving and growing, see life from an eternal perspective, and obedient.

Again, do you really want to be the woman God has called you to be?

Let me summarize the ten steps of moving from an insecure woman to a woman of impact:

1. **Do consistent self-check:** Ask yourself personal questions to evaluate your decisions, behaviors, and beliefs. Ensure your character, thoughts, motives, and actions are aligned with God.

2. **Repent:** Confess and turn away from anything displeasing to God, and that leads you to sin, disappointment, and disobedience.

3. **Renew Your Mind:** Let go of the old way of thinking and embrace godly thoughts about yourself, your purpose, and your future.

4. **Get God's Vision:** Stop limiting yourself but see and accept that God's plan for you is greater and nothing you have done can disqualify His purpose for your life.

5. **Pray, Fast, and Get Deliverance:** Praying is speaking to God about your life, struggles, and dreams. Fasting requires giving up something for a period of time, and spending time seeking God for specific things. Deliverance is necessary because sometimes things are so deep-rooted that we have to cast out spirits that hinder our destiny.

6. **Take faith steps:** Faith says I believe God, and I am taking action to prove I believe. You take the first step even when you do not see the entire staircase.

7. **Affirm what God says about you:** Read your Bible, recite God's promises over your life, declare them boldly by saying them out loud, writing them down, and repeating the words until you believe them.

8. **Serve others with your gifts:** Do not bury or underplay your gifts; put them to work. Support others by sharing your abilities, passions, and talents to bless others.

9. **Keep an eternal perspective:** This means reminding yourself that life on earth is temporary, so how you waste or invest your time, resources, or gifts will not only impact life now but also in eternity. It helps us to focus on God's grace, hope, love, mercy, and faith and not only on our current circumstances.

10. **Remember, it is not about you: Insecurities plague us because we tend to live such a** self-focused life, which leads to constant discouragement and comparison. This statement is counter-cultural because everything about the world teaches us about self-love, self-care, self-fulfillment, self-motivation, etc. In Rick Warren's book, Purpose-Driven life, I was challenged to truly remind myself that this life is about GOD. While it is nice to accomplish things and feel satisfied, at the end of the day, my life, your life, should bring God glory. Only when we focus on Jesus Christ will insecurities dissipate, self-doubts fade, and gifts become activated to impact and leave a lasting legacy.

Chapter 16

# How To Consistently Overcome Insecurity

The truth is, you cannot read this book once and think all your insecurities will just disappear. These feelings of self-doubt, fear, or anxiety were built over the years, so it will take you daily choosing and practicing these habits to become more confident and courageous in your calling.

I cannot end this book without talking about the power of the Holy Spirit. Many times, believers put limitations on their gifts because they quench the Holy Spirit or do not acknowledge Him enough.

True boldness... Impacting Boldness... Transformational Boldness can ONLY come through the power of the Holy Spirit.

**Dear Insecurity**

*Now when they saw the boldness of Peter and John, and perceived that they were uneducated, common men, they were astonished (Acts 4:13 - ESV).*

*And now, Lord, look upon their threats and grant to your servants to continue to speak your word with all boldness (Acts 4:29 - ESV).*

*And they were all filled with the Holy Spirit and continued to speak the word of God with boldness (Acts 4:31 - ESV).*

So, every time you feel like insecurity is trying to get a hold of you again, ask the Holy Spirit to empower you and give you the boldness you need to truly fulfill your purpose, activate your gifts, and become who God has truly called you to be.

Let us start now. Write a letter to Him today!

Dear Holy Spirit,

_____

_____

_____

_____

_____

_____

_____

_____

# Conclusion

I am happy you chose this book. Why? Because many believers are only concerned about getting saved to go to heaven and not realize that there is more to life (after salvation).

God has created and called you for a purpose, and that purpose includes using your gifts to bless others and bring Him glory.

Let me repeat, so you can read slowly (sometimes we read books for entertainment or inspiration but never allow the lessons to be activated in our lives to do something about it.)

_____ (insert your name) if you are a Christian (believer in Jesus Christ), God has a purpose for your life, even before He created you and placed you on this earth. Jesus' blood not only saved you from death (separation from God), but He saved you to have life more abundantly (experiences when we truly use our gifts/message) to bless and serve each other.

If God saved you just to go to heaven, you would have died when you accepted the gift of salvation. But, we did not die because God has a good plan for us. Therefore, everything you have been through (your story), everything He has blessed you

### Dear Insecurity

with (gifts), and all the lessons you have learnt (message), are to impact others (if you use them and share it).

Here is my challenge to you after reading this book:

- Pray about your spiritual gifts and start looking at places you can serve (it can be in church, workplace, school, business, community, etc.)

- Journal the top three action steps you will take from the lessons you learnt (show your faith by taking action).

- Encourage a friend to get a copy of the book too (or get them a gift), so you can have someone to discuss it with and keep you accountable for when taking your faith-steps (sharing is caring).

- Complete the Insecurity to Impact 7-Day Challenge at the end of this book. (I believe you will have a life-changing experience, knowing you have been a blessing to others).

- Finally, send me an email at info@crystaldaye.com with subject line: Dear Insecurity to share your breakthroughs, lessons, testimonies, and prayer requests.

If you are still struggling with the concept of purpose, please, if you haven't yet, go get a copy of my books *Living A Royal Reality* and *Empowered For Such A Time As This*.

If you are struggling with growing deeper in intimacy with God so you can hear His voice, get a copy of my book, *Draw Closer To God Devotional*.

**I love you, and God loves you more.**
**Crystal**

# 7 DAY FROM INSECURITY TO IMPACT CHALLENGE

## DAY 1

Do a spiritual gifts test (you can find them on Google) and journal how you can use your gifts to make an impact.

**Journal Day 1 Take-Away**

_____
_____
_____
_____
_____
_____
_____
_____
_____
_____
_____
_____
_____
_____
_____
_____
_____
_____
_____

## DAY 2

Today, do something that scares you. Evangelize to a loved one, start a conversation with a stranger, volunteer to speak in public, or do a live video.

Remember, courage is not the absence of fear; it is moving ahead in spite of fear.

**Journal Day 2 Take-Away**

_____
_____
_____
_____
_____
_____
_____
_____
_____
_____
_____
_____
_____
_____
_____
_____

## DAY 3

Read a scripture outline, then pray out loud. Most times, we read the Bible in our minds and pray in our minds.

Today, choose to read a full chapter out loud then pray out loud.

**Journal Day 3 Take-Away**

## DAY 4

Plan a community service activity and be intentional about going into your community to help someone less fortunate.

**Journal Day 4 Take-Away**

## DAY 5

Commit to ending something that is not serving you. For example, stop the negative self-talk, do not spend any money on things emotionally, let go of an unhealthy relationship, and unfollow anyone you feel is jealous of or who you compare yourself to.

**Journal Day 5 Take-Away**

## DAY 6

Do something nice for someone else that costs you. Buy dinner for a friend, pay for the person next in line at the supermarket, visit an elderly, purchase lunch for a homeless person, etc.

**Journal Day 6 Take-Away**

_____
_____
_____
_____
_____
_____
_____
_____
_____
_____
_____
_____
_____
_____
_____
_____
_____
_____

## DAY 7

Every day for the next seven days, look in the mirror and tell yourself what God says about you. Write down scriptures and remind yourself that you belong to God.

**Journal Day 7 Take-away**

_____
_____
_____
_____
_____
_____
_____
_____
_____
_____
_____
_____
_____
_____
_____
_____
_____
_____
_____
_____

impact lives globally. She has a genuine passion for supporting the spiritual, personal, and entrepreneurial development of women all over the world.

Crystal is a Book Coach and CEO of DayeLight Publishers, a Faith-Based Publishing and Consultancy Company that is aspiring authors to write, brand, publish and market the books God has placed on their hearts so they can impact the next generation.

As Brand Strategist and Business Coach, she helps women of faith to turn their experiences into an empowerment-based business. She teaches kingdom solopreneurs to monetize their message and build a profitable brand and business God's way. She believes her life's mission is to inspire and equip women to live wholesome godly lives while increasing their impact and income. She motivates people daily through her writing, speaking, coaching, and mentoring, with the aim of empowering aspiring leaders so they can empower others.

To connect with Crystal, visit her website at www.crystaldaye.com or www.dayelightpublishers.com and follow her on IG, FB, and LinkedIn. For booking, contact info@crystaldaye.com

# About The Author

Known to captivate and connect with people as a relevant, transparent, and transformational speaker, Crystal Daye propels her audience to action by challenging them to never settle for less than God's best.

Crystal Daye is an international certified Christian Life Coach, Corporate Trainer, host of the "Diary of a Jesus Girl Podcast," kingdom influencer, and Christelle's mother. As a woman of faith, she believes in servant leadership. She unselfishly uses the platforms God has given her to positively influence and impact lives globally. She has a genuine passion for supporting the spiritual, personal, and entrepreneurial development of women all over the world.

Crystal is a Book Coach and CEO of DayeLight Publishers, a Faith-Based Publishing and Consultancy Company that is aspiring authors to write, brand, publish and market the books God has placed on their hearts so they can impact the next generation.

As Brand Strategist and Business Coach, she helps women of faith to turn their experiences into an empowerment-based business. She teaches kingdom solopreneurs to monetize their message and build a profitable brand and business God's way. She believes her life's mission is to inspire and equip women to live wholesome godly lives while increasing their impact and income. She motivates people daily through her writing, speaking, coaching, and mentoring, with the aim of empowering aspiring leaders so they can empower others.

To connect with Crystal, visit her website at www.crystaldaye.com or www.dayelightpublishers.com and follow her on IG, FB, and LinkedIn. For booking, contact info@crystaldaye.com

www.ingramcontent.com/pod-product-compliance
Lightning Source LLC
Chambersburg PA
CBHW021426070526
**44577CB00001B/75**